Watching the Weather

Forecasting the Weather

Elizabeth Miles

Heinemann Library
Chicago, Illinois

Designed by Richard Parker and Q2A Solutions
Illustrations: Jeff Edwards
Originated by Dot Gradations Ltd.
Printed and bound in China by South China Printing Company

09 08 07 06 05
10 9 8 7 6 5 4 3 2 1

Library of Congress Cataloging-in-Publication Data
Miles, Elizabeth, 1960-
    Forecasting the weather / Elizabeth Miles.
        p. cm. -- (Watching the weather)
    Includes bibliographical references and index.
    ISBN 1-4034-6553-3 -- ISBN 1-4034-6558-4 (pbk.)
1. Weather forecasting--Juvenile literature. I. Title. II. Series.
    QC995.43.M55 2003
    551.63--dc22
                                    2004018490

Acknowledgments
The Publishers would like to thank the following for permission to reproduce photographs: Alamy pp. **7** (Robert Harding World Imagery), **24** (The Photo Library Wales); Corbis pp. **13** (Paul Seheult/Eye Ubiquitous), **15**, **17** (Craig Tuttle), **20** (Michael S Yamashita), **26** (Reuters); Digital Vision p. **6**; Harcourt Education Ltd p. **21** (Peter Evans); Masterfile p. **11** (Bill Frymire); NASA pp. **18**, **19**; P A Photos p. **22** (DPA); Reuters pp. **23** (Peter Jones), **27** (David Loh); Rex Features p. **4** (DCY); Robert Harding Picture Library p.**5**; Science Photo Library pp. **8** (British Antarctic Survey), **9** (Phillippe Psaila); Topham Picturepoint pp. **10** (Image Works), **25**; Tudor Photography pp. **28**, **29**.

Cover photograph of a meteorologist attending to the Doppler Weather Radar, reproduced with permission of Corbis/Brownie Harris.

The Publishers would like to thank Daniel Ogden for his assistance in the preparation of this book.

Contents

Some words are shown in bold, **like this**. You can find out what they mean by looking in the glossary.

What Is a Weather Forecast?

The weather often changes. It might rain or snow. It might feel hot or cold. A weather **forecast** tells you what the weather might be in the future.

This weather forecast says it is going to rain.

Short-term forecasts might tell you what tomorrow's weather will be. They might also say what the weather will be for the next few days.

If rain is forecast, you might need to wear a raincoat or carry an umbrella.

Who Needs a Weather Forecast?

The weather affects everyone. If hot weather is **forecast**, people can keep cool by putting on light summer clothes. They might plan a day out in the sunshine.

If a sunny day is forecast, people might choose to go on a picnic.

Fishers will not go to sea if they know a dangerous storm is on its way.

If cold weather is forecast, people wear thick, warm clothes. If ice is forecast, people might stay indoors to avoid slippery roads.

How Do We Forecast the Weather?

To figure out what the weather will be, **forecasters** need information from different places. Computers help collect this information.

Weather balloons are released all around the world. They gather information from high in the sky.

Gathering information helps forecasters to understand what the weather is now. This also helps them figure out what the weather will be in the future.

Instruments at **weather stations** gather information, such as the direction of the wind.

Weather Maps

Weather maps can show many things, such as which way warm or cold air is moving.

Forecasters produce weather **maps** to tell people about the weather. The maps show what the weather is now or what it will be in the future.

Some weather maps show lots of information. Other weather maps are simpler and easier to understand.

Pictures on this weather map show where it will be sunny, cloudy, or stormy.

Air Pressure

Meteorologists measure air pressure to help figure out what the weather will be. Air pressure tells us if the air is rising or sinking.

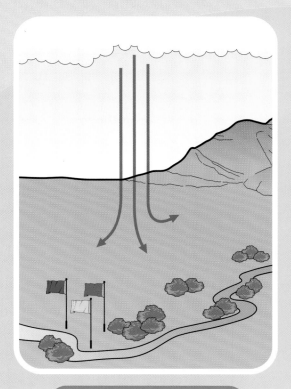

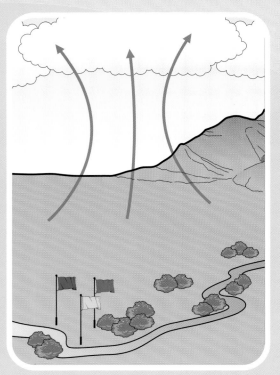

When there is high pressure, the air is sinking.

When there is low pressure, the air is rising.

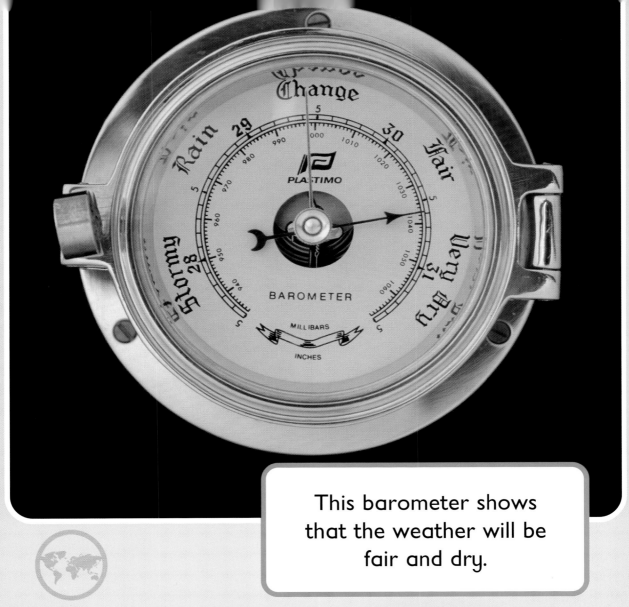

This barometer shows that the weather will be fair and dry.

Meteorologists use an instrument called a barometer to measure air pressure. Some barometers show what kind of weather to expect.

Highs and Lows

If there is high air pressure coming, calm weather is often **forecast**. In summer, this often means that the weather will be mild and clear.

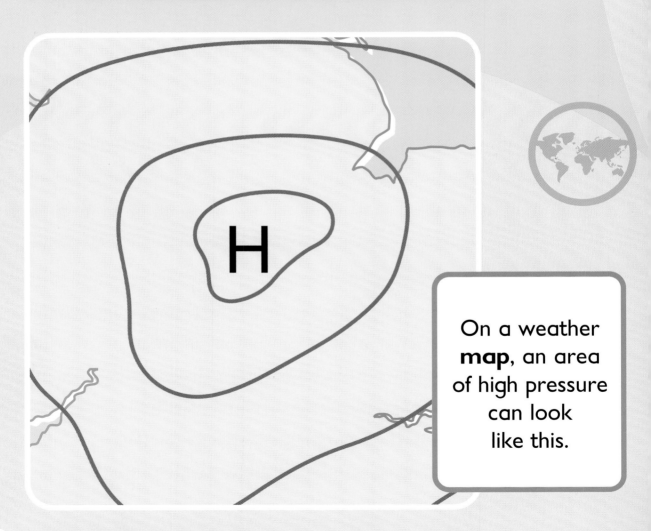

On a weather **map**, an area of high pressure can look like this.

When the air pressure is low, it often means rainy and windy weather.

Low air pressure can mean that the weather will be stormy, wet, and windy. The sky often will be cloudy.

Weather Fronts

A weather front is where two **masses** of air meet. A warm front is where warm air moves toward colder air. A cold front is cold air moving toward warmer air.

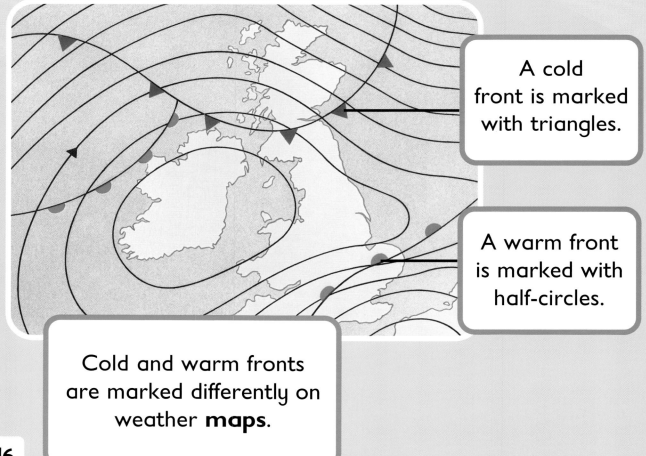

A cold front is marked with triangles.

A warm front is marked with half-circles.

Cold and warm fronts are marked differently on weather **maps**.

Cirrus clouds can be the first sign of a warm front moving in.

Fronts can bring cloudy, rainy weather. By watching where fronts are going, the weather **forecaster** can figure out where it might rain.

Following a Storm

Meteorologists can **forecast** a storm by looking at photographs taken from space. They can see if storm clouds are developing over the sea.

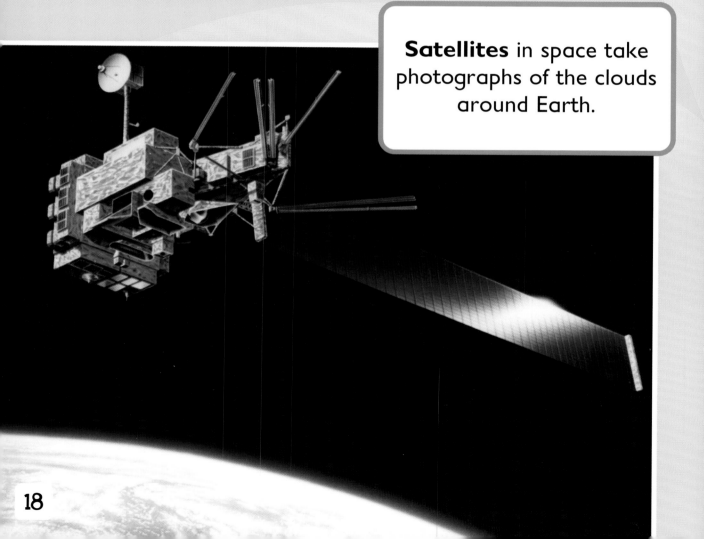

Satellites in space take photographs of the clouds around Earth.

Satellite photographs show how strong a storm might be. This storm is a **hurricane**.

Meteorologists can measure the wind and figure out which way a storm is going. A weather forecast tells people living nearby when the storm might reach them.

Looking at the Clouds

Towering black clouds called cumulonimbus can bring thunder and lightning.

You can sometimes **forecast** the local weather by looking at the clouds. Different kinds of clouds bring different types of weather.

Dark, low-lying clouds bring wet weather.

When low-level clouds begin to cover the sky, it might soon begin to rain or snow. Clouds called nimbostratus can bring long periods of rain.

Weather Warnings

Forecasters warn people if dangerous weather is on the way. Airplane flights might have to be cancelled. People might stay indoors if snow or ice is **forecast**.

Snow and ice make roads dangerous. Signs warn drivers to slow down.

Shelters like this help protect people from dangerous storms.

Tornadoes and **hurricanes** can be more dangerous if they come as a surprise. If people are warned, they can take **shelter** before the storm arrives.

Animals and Plants

Animals and plants need to stay safe during bad weather. If snow is **forecast**, farmers make sure their animals have food and do not get stuck in **snowdrifts**.

If snow is forecast, farmers may bring their sheep down from the hills, closer to the farm.

Farmers may put special tents over their crops to protect them from frost.

Frost can kill many plants. If freezing cold weather is forecast, gardeners try to protect their **crops**. To keep the plants warm, they might wrap them in plastic or take them indoors.

Disaster: Surprise Storm

Weather **forecasts** are not always right. It is difficult to know how strong a storm will be. It is also hard to figure out where a storm will go.

A change of wind direction can bring a surprise storm.

Weeks of dry weather can dry out the soil and cause plants to die.

Long-term forecasts are hard to make. It is difficult to figure out how long a type of weather will last.

Project: Are They Right?

Now that you have learned all about weather **forecast**s, you can check to see how many are right!

You will need:
- white card
- scissors
- colored felt-tipped pens
- tape or putty

1. On the card, draw and color a simple **map** of your area.

2. Make colored card symbols for all the main weather types.
3. For a week, in the morning watch or listen to a local weather forecast. Use your map to record what the forecasters say the weather will be that day. Stick the right symbols on your map using the tape or putty.
4. Each day, compare the weather outside with your weather map.
5. Were the weather forecasts right?

Glossary

crop plant grown for food or to sell, such as vegetables and fruit

forecast try to figure out what the weather will be in the future

forecaster person who figures out what the weather might be

frost frozen water vapor close to the ground

hurricane storm with very strong winds and heavy rain

map drawing of all or part of an area

mass large area of air

meteorologist person who studies the weather

satellite spacecraft that goes around Earth and carries equipment such as cameras

shelter strong building, built to keep people safe in very strong winds

snowdrift thick snow that piles up in the wind

tornado storm with winds that spin very fast

weather balloon balloon that carries weather instruments high into the sky

weather station building where air, wind, and cloud measurements are taken and recorded

More Books to Read

Hughes, Monica. *Nature's Patterns: Weather Patterns.* Chicago: Heinemann Library, 2004.

Rodgers, Alan, and Streluk, Angela. *Measuring the Weather: Forecasting Weather.* Chicago: Heinemann Library, 2002.

Simon, Seymour. *Weather.* New York: HarperTrophy, 2000.

Index